Hal Leonard Student Piano Library

Notespeller for Piano

A Visit to *Music City*
with Spike and Party Cat

Book 3
and Book 4 Exercises
Revised Edition

Author
Karen Harrington

Illustrator
Fred Bell

FOREWORD

The **Notespeller for Piano** presents note-recognition activities that coordinate with the **Piano Lessons** books in the **Hal Leonard Student Piano Library**.

Students join Spike and Party Cat as they explore the sights and tourist attractions in *Music City*. Their visit includes assignments that help students sharpen their music reading skills, learn to read ledger-line notes, and identify intervals, half and whole steps, and major/minor five-finger patterns.

Best wishes,

Karen Harrington

ISBN 978-0-634-03025-3

HAL•LEONARD®

Visit Hal Leonard Online at
www.halleonard.com

World headquarters, contact:
Hal Leonard
7777 West Bluemound Road
Milwaukee, WI 53213
Email: info@halleonard.com

In Europe, contact:
Hal Leonard Europe Limited
1 Red Place
London, W1K 6PL
Email: info@halleonardeurope.com

In Australia, contact:
Hal Leonard Australia Pty. Ltd.
4 Lentara Court
Cheltenham, Victoria, 3192 Australia
Email: info@halleonard.com.au

Rhythm Train Terminal

Spike and Party Cat are excited about their trip to *Music City*. As they ride the train into the city, they talk about the sights they plan to see during their stay.

Name the notes to discover their sightseeing plans.

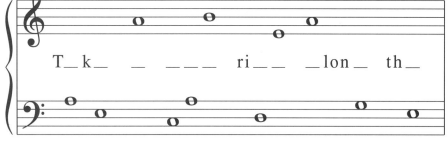

T_k_ _ ___ ri__ _lon_ th_

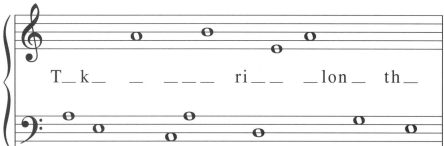

St_ ____to Isl_n_ _r__w_y.

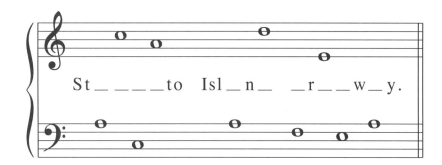

W_lk __ross ___thov_n _ri___.

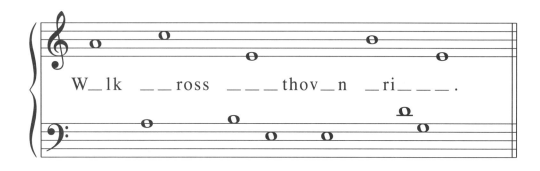

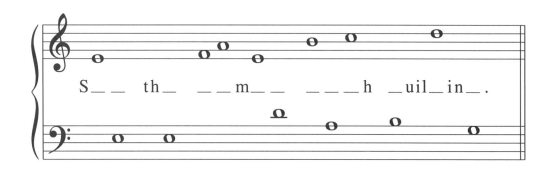

S__ th_ __m__ ___h _uil_in_.

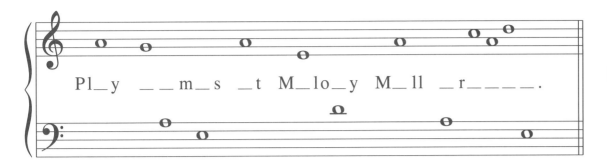

Pl_y _ _m_s _t M_lo_y M_ll _r_ _ _ _.

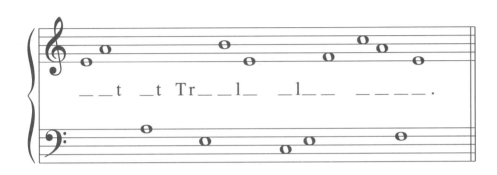

_ _t _t Tr_ _l_ _l_ _ _ _ _.

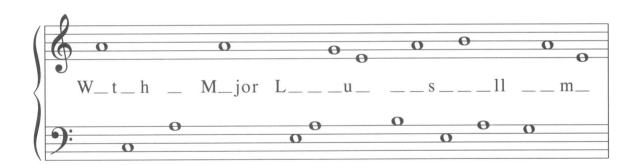

W_t_h _ M_jor L_ _ _u_ _ _s_ _ _ll _ _m_

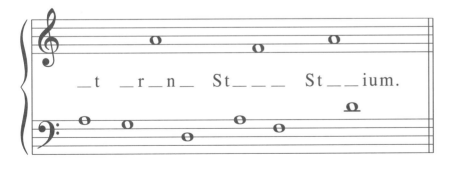

_t _r_n_ St_ _ _ St_ _ium.

Half-Note Hotel

During their visit to *Music City*, Spike and Party Cat are staying in a room on the 5th floor at the Half-Note Hotel.

1. Draw half notes a 5th up or down from the note in each window.
2. Write the note names in the blue boxes.

A Cab Ride to the Music City Zoo

Spike and Party Cat take a *cab* ride to the Music City Zoo. At the zoo they will have a brown *bag* lunch and *gab* while watching the *caged* animals.

Draw half notes in the large blue boxes on each staff to spell the word at the top of each column in three different places.

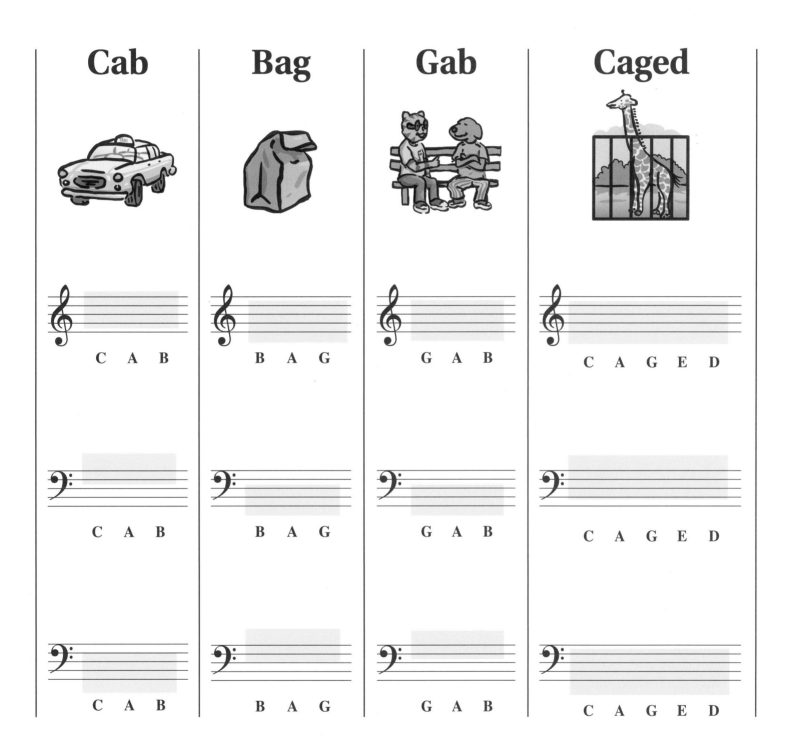

Use with Lesson Book 3, pg. 6

Dinner at Six

Spike and Party Cat will have dinner at 6:00 p.m. and then see a musical in the city's theater district.

1. Draw half notes or quarter notes a 6th up or down from the note on each dinner table.
2. Write the note names in the blue boxes.

Who Wants to Be a Musician?

Spike and Party Cat audition for the popular TV game show, *Who Wants to Be a Musician?* Party Cat is chosen as a contestant! Answer these questions to find out what he has won.

If you don't know the answer, you have three options:

1. Look on your piano.   2. Ask your teacher.   3. Phone a friend.

For **$60,000**, name these *ascending* intervals. Each answer is worth $15,000.

1. C   up to   G   ☐
2. G   up to   C   ☐
3. D   up to   F   ☐
4. F   up to   D   ☐

For **$120,000**, name these *descending* intervals. Each answer is worth $30,000.

1. D   down to   F   ☐
2. F   down to   D   ☐
3. G   down to   C   ☐
4. C   down to   G   ☐

For **$300,000**, answer each of these questions correctly. Each answer is worth $150,000.

1. This interval has two white keys between the first key and the last key.   ☐

2. This interval has three white keys between the first key and the last key.   ☐

For the **Grand Prize** of **$1,000,000**, Party Cat may choose to answer the last question or stop and leave with his winnings. Follow the instructions below to find out what he did.

H

1. D   up a 6th and down a 5th   ☐
2. C   up a 3rd and down a 2nd   ☐
3. F   down a 5th and up a 4th   ☐
4. B   up a 4th and down a 3rd   ☐

i

5. A   down a 6th and up a 2nd   ☐
6. D   up a 4th and down a 3rd   ☐
7. E   down a 5th and up a 4th   ☐

t
o

8. F   up a 6th and down a 5th   ☐

o

9. C   down a 6th and up a 2nd   ☐

o
r

i
t

7

The J.S. Bach Building

Name these notes to complete the story.

Party Cat and Spike were ▢ x ▢ it ▢ ▢ about their visit to the

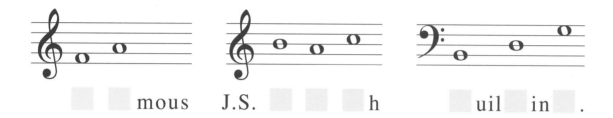

▢ ▢ mous   J.S. ▢ ▢ h   ▢ uil ▢ in ▢ .

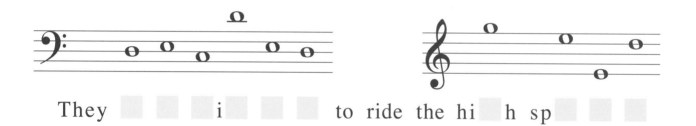

They ▢ ▢ ▢ i ▢ ▢ to ride the hi ▢ h sp ▢ ▢ ▢

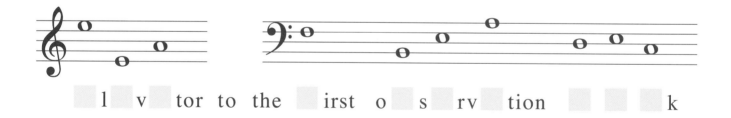

▢ l ▢ v ▢ tor to the ▢ irst o ▢ s ▢ rv ▢ tion ▢ ▢ k

on the ▢ i ▢ ty- ▢ i ▢ th ▢ loor.

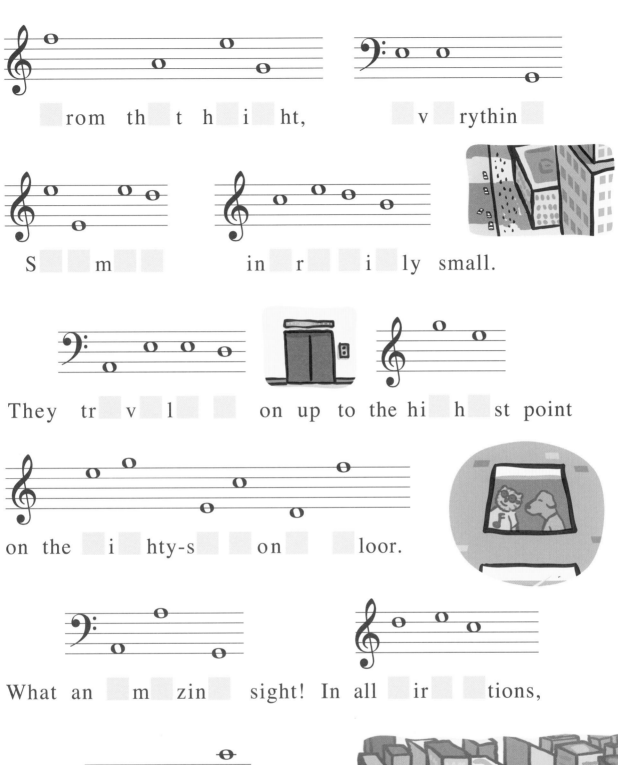

▢rom th▢t h▢i▢ht, ▢v▢rythin▢

S▢▢m▢▢ in r▢▢i▢ly small.

They tr▢v▢l▢▢ on up to the hi▢h▢st point

on the ▢i▢hty-s▢▢on▢ ▢loor.

What an ▢m▢zin▢ sight! In all ▢ir▢▢tions,

the view o▢ th▢ ▢ity

was ▢r▢▢tht▢kin▢.

Treble-Clef Café

Having lunch or dinner at the famous Treble-Clef Café is a special treat. The walls are decorated with all sorts of musical instruments, and the food is great.

Some of the items on the menu are listed in the crossword puzzle below.
1. Solve the crossword clues by naming the notes.
2. Complete the crossword puzzle.

Across

3. _ _ _ on _ n _ _ _ _ _ s

6. _ _ _ _ _ _ _ _ rolls

10. _ r _ _ _ _

11. _ _ k _ _ _ _ u _ _ _

12. _ h _ _ s _ n _ _ hos

13. _ r _ n _ h _ ri _ s

Down

1. _ ho _ ol _ t _ _ _ k _

2. _ h _ _ s _ _ ur _ _ r

4. _ r _ _ k _ _ ss _ rol _

5. v _ _ _ t _ _ l _ s

7. _ _ r _ _ _ u _

8. _ _ _ _ k _ _ o _ s

9. _ ri _ _ _ _ hi _ k _ n

Grand Staff Stadium

You can't visit *Music City* without taking in a baseball game played by the Bass Clef Bears. As each batter comes up to bat and hits a ball, it flies out into a different part of the outfield.

1. Write the note names in the blue boxes for each whole note.
2. Draw a line connecting each note to the correct outfield area by matching it to the correct key on the keyboard.
3. Add a stem to each note, turning the whole notes into half notes.

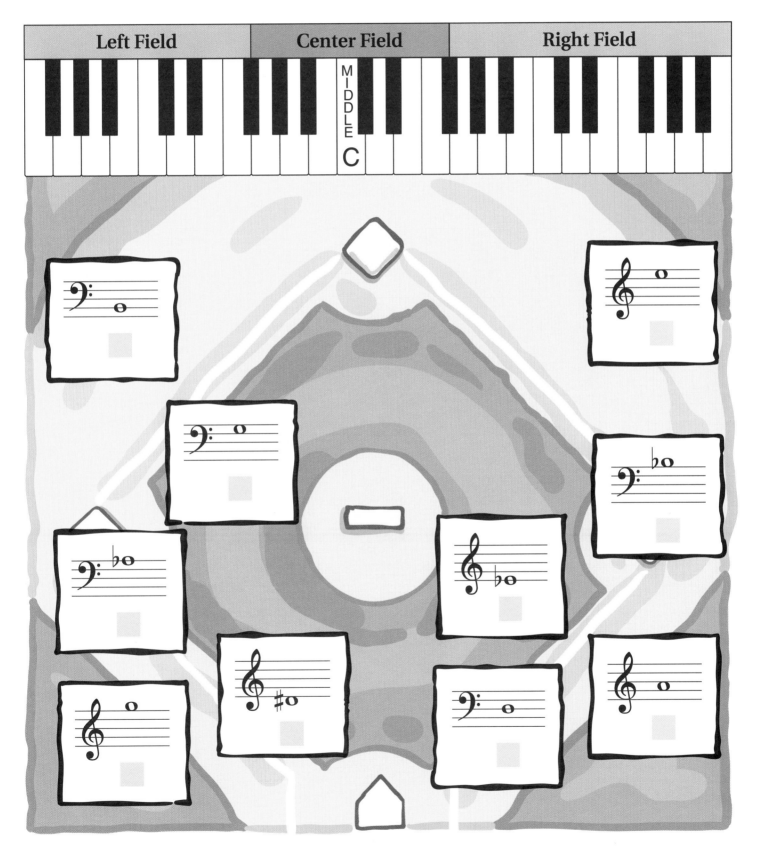

Use with Lesson Book 3, pg. 20

Steppin' Out in Harmony Village

Spike and Party Cat enjoy their walking tour through Harmony Village. The streets are lined with interesting buildings: churches, art galleries, townhouses, coffeehouses and shops. Many artists, writers, poets, musicians and actors live in this historic part of *Music City*.

1. Write the note names in the blue boxes.
2. Write "H" (half step) or "W" (whole step) in the blank below each pair of notes.

Follow the directions to draw and name the notes below:

Up a half step

Up a whole step

Down a whole step

Down a half step

Up a whole step

Down a whole step

Down a half step

Up a half step

The Beethoven Bridge

Walking across Beethoven Bridge is a real treat! From the bridge you can see the whole skyline of *Music City*. The Ferry Boat also passes under the bridge on the way up the river. In the evening you can see the bright, neon lights of the Wonder Wheel on Staccato Island.

1. Draw whole notes for each major five-finger pattern from each starting note on the grand staves below.
2. Write the note names in the blue boxes.

Draw and name the notes in *descending* order for each major 5-finger pattern below.

Use with Lesson Book 3, pgs. 24-42

Music City Ferry-Boat Tour

Party Cat and Spike ride the Music City Ferry Boat to see the city from the river. The boat will pass the downtown skyscrapers, Harmony Village, Jazz Town, and the amusement park on Staccato Island.

1. Write the note names in the blue boxes.
2. Draw a line from each major five-finger pattern to the letter name on the boat that matches it.

Use with Lesson Book 3, pgs. 24-42

The Haydn Planetarium

The Space Theater at the world-famous Haydn Planetarium presents views of our night sky that are so realistic, visitors feel as though they have been sent into space.

1. Draw whole notes moving up or down by 3rds from each given note.
2. Write the note names in the blue boxes.
3. Draw a line to match each major triad in the left column to the same triad in the right column.

Space Notes Moving Up

Space Notes Moving Down

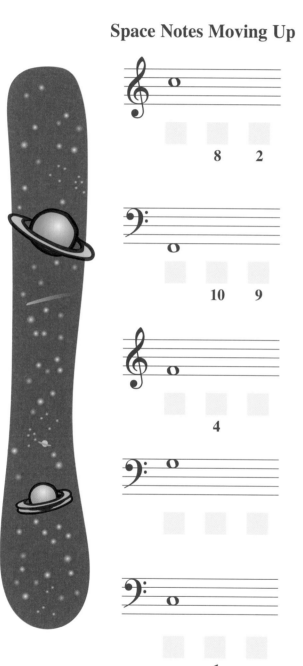

8   2

10   9

4

1

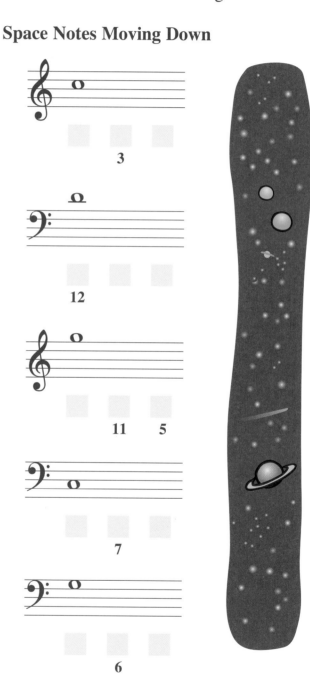

3

12

11   5

7

6

Match the numbered letters above with the numbered lines below to find the definition of *Milky Way*.

Th___ ___ ___l___xy in whi___h th___ sol___r syst___m is lo___ ___t___ ___.
  1   2   3   4   5   6   7   8   9 10 11 12

Staccato Island Freeway

Along the Staccato Island Freeway, Spike and Party Cat see billboards advertising minor five-finger patterns.

1. Draw whole notes for each minor five-finger pattern from each starting note on the grand staves below.
2. Write the note names in the blue boxes.

Draw and name the notes in *descending* order for each minor five-finger pattern below.

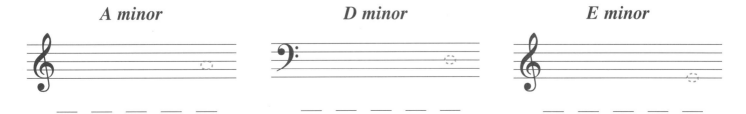

Use with Lesson Book 3, pgs. 28-45

The Wonder Wheel

Staccato Island is the most popular amusement park in *Music City*. Party Cat and Spike are eager to ride the famous Wonder Wheel, a ferris wheel that towers 150 feet high.

1. Write the note names in the blue boxes on each ferris-wheel car.
2. Draw a straight line from the five-finger pattern on each car to the letter name on the center circle that matches it.

Tune-Time Trolley

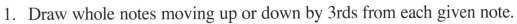

Spike and Party Cat enjoy riding the trolley to get around *Music City*. As long as they know which trolley line to take, they can go almost anywhere in the city.

1. Draw whole notes moving up or down by 3rds from each given note.
2. Write the note names in the blue boxes.
3. Draw a line to match each minor triad in the left column to the same triad in the right column.

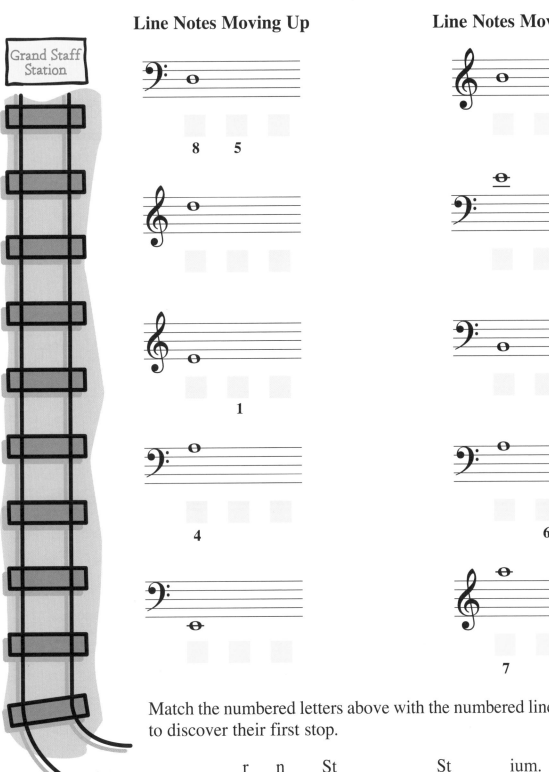

Line Notes Moving Up

8   5

1

4

Line Notes Moving Down

2

6   3

7

Match the numbered letters above with the numbered lines below to discover their first stop.

___r___n___ St___ ___ ___ St___ ___ium.
 1   2   3   4   5   6   7   8

Use with Lesson Book 3, pgs. 28-45

Flags Along Sonatina Street

Colorful flags fly high all along Sonatina Street.
Draw whole notes on each flag, using only these treble-clef notes:

Choose letters from the blue boxes to discover a special *Music City* event.
Each letter is used only once.

__ o n __ __ r t __ t M __ l o __ y M __ l l

Symphony Park

Symphony Park, in the very heart of *Music City*, is famous for its beautiful landscapes and gardens. Spike and Party Cat enjoy a brief rest from the bustle of the city here, watching people at play.

Many outdoor activities that people enjoy are listed in the crossword puzzle below.
1. Solve the crossword clues by naming the notes.
2. Complete the crossword puzzle.

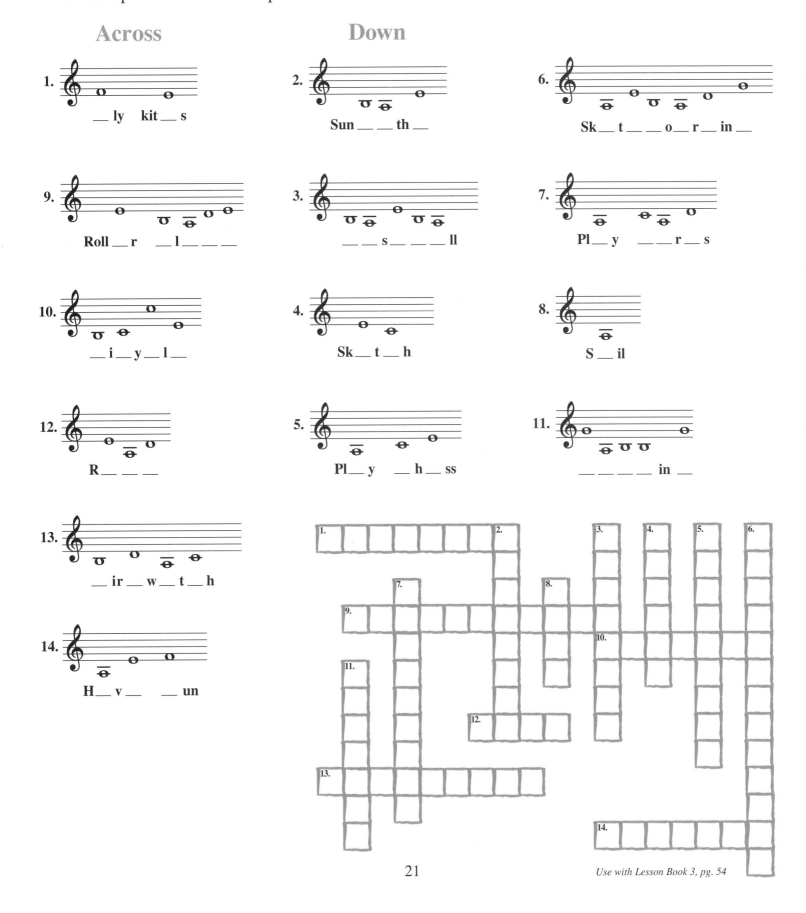

Across

1. __ ly   kit __ s

9. Roll __ r   __ l __ __ __

10. __ i __ y __ l __

12. R __ __ __

13. __ ir __ w __ t __ h

14. H __ v __   __ un

Down

2. Sun __ __ th __

3. __ __ s __ __ __ ll

4. Sk __ t __ h

5. Pl __ y   __ h __ ss

6. Sk __ t __ __ o __ r __ in __

7. Pl __ y   __ __ r __ s

8. S __ il

11. __ __ __ __   in __

Use with Lesson Book 3, pg. 54

Orchestra Hall

At Symphony Park, Spike and Party Cat meet some singers who are in town for a choral festival. They invite Party Cat and Spike to join them for a grand performance that evening at Orchestra Hall. Below is the festival theme song, *Many Voices*.

1. Circle all the 7ths in the student part and then play each one.
2. Play and sing *Many Voices* with your teacher.

Many Voices

Joyous March

f Man - y voic - es com - ing to-geth - er, hear our an-thems ring.

cel - e - brat-ing mu - sic with songs that we love to sing.

Accompaniment (Student plays one octave higher.)

With pedal

mf When we raise our voic - es to - geth - er, stand-ing side by side,

f we cre - ate a spir - it that fills each heart with pride!

The World Art Museum

One of the sights Spike and Party Cat can't miss is the World Art Museum with its vast treasures from around the world. This famous museum hosts many exhibits devoted to special collections.

Name the notes on each frame to find out what exhibits Spike and Party Cat will see.

Legato Lake Festival

Spike and Party Cat take a side trip to Legato Lake Park where a lakefront festival is being held. They rent a rowboat and enjoy a relaxing time out on the lake. As Spike and Party Cat lazily drift around the lake in their boat, they decide to play a game about 7ths and octaves. You can play too!

On each staff below, draw 7ths or octaves up or down from the given note.

Write 7ths going up.	**Write octaves going up.**	**Write 7ths going down.**	**Write octaves going down.**

Use with Lesson Book 4, pg. 24

Festival Games

At the lakefront festival, Spike and Party Cat try their luck tossing rings around bottles.

1st (Unison), 3rd, 5th, 7th: These intervals go from *line to line*, or *space to space*.

1. Write the note names in the blue boxes.
2. Draw a line from each ring to the correct interval name on the bottles.

Time To Eat!

At a festival snack bar, Spike and Party Cat order their favorite sandwiches and sodas. The sandwiches have 2nds, 4ths, 6ths, and 8ths (octaves) on them.

> **2nd, 4th, 6th, 8th (octave):** These intervals go from *line to space,* or *space to line.*

1. Write the note names in the blue boxes.
2. Draw a line from each sandwich to the correct interval name on the soda cups.

4/4 **Time Square**

Name these bass-staff notes to complete the story.

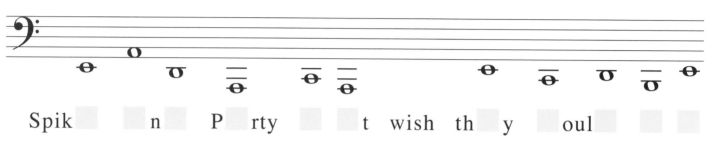

Spik n P rty t wish th y oul

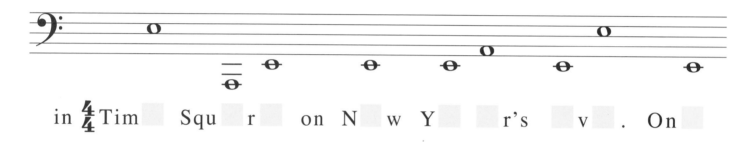

in **4/4** Tim Squ r on N w Y r's v . On

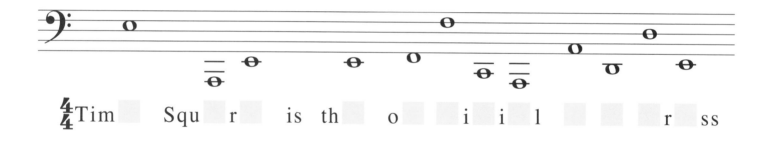

4/4 Tim Squ r is th o i i l r ss

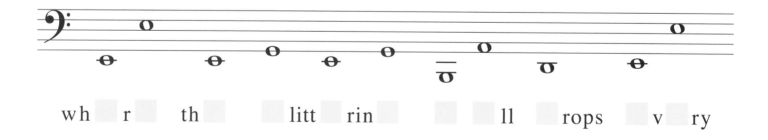

wh r th litt rin ll rops v ry

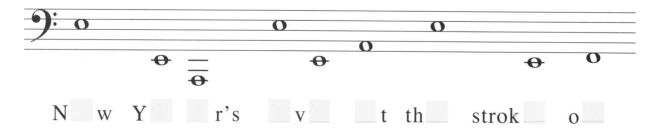

N w Y r's v t th strok o

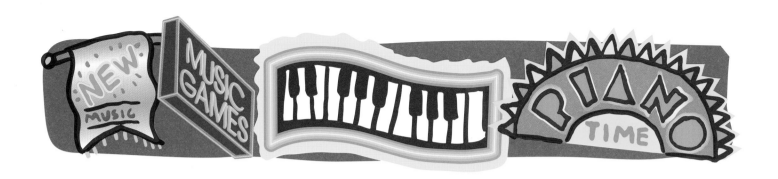

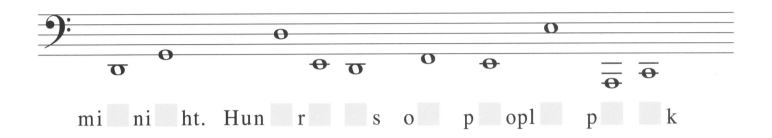

mi ni ht. Hun r s o p opl p k

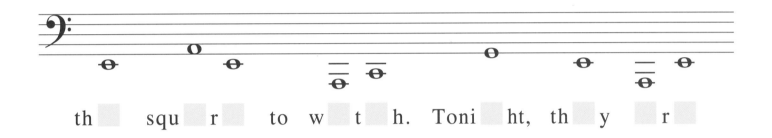

th squ r to w t h. Toni ht, th y r

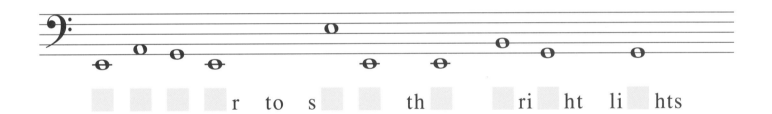

r to s th ri ht li hts

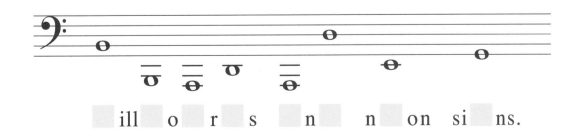

o th mous l troni

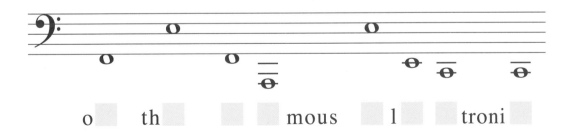

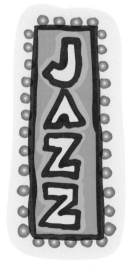

ill o r s n n on si ns.

Mozart Center for the Performing Arts

The Mozart Center for the Performing Arts is a large arts complex for music, opera, theater, and dance performances. The halls in the center are named below.

Draw a quarter note to match each note name in the blue boxes, using only these bass-clef notes:

C entr a l C ity Op e r a

B a ch Re c it a l H a ll

F in e A rts Th e a t e r

G r e a t H a ll f or B a ll e t

Son a tin a S c hool f or Pi a nists

Melody Mall

The 'in' place to shop in *Music City* is Melody Mall.
On the last day of their visit, Party Cat and Spike spend
a great afternoon there doing many fun things.

Name the notes on each staff to discover what they do at the mall.

1.

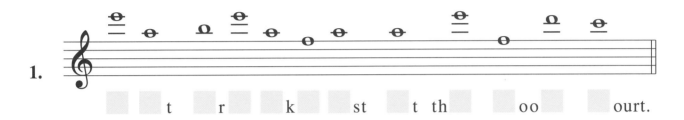

☐ t ☐ r ☐ k ☐ st ☐ t ☐ th ☐ oo ☐ ourt.

2.

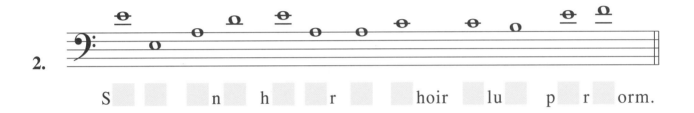

S ☐ ☐ n ☐ h ☐ r ☐ hoir ☐ lu ☐ p ☐ r ☐ orm.

3.

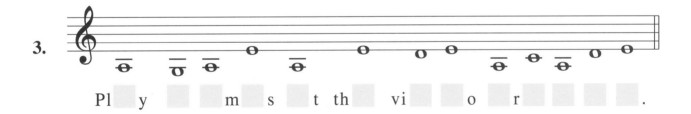

Pl ☐ y ☐ ☐ m ☐ s ☐ t th ☐ vi ☐ o ☐ r ☐ ☐ ☐ .

4.

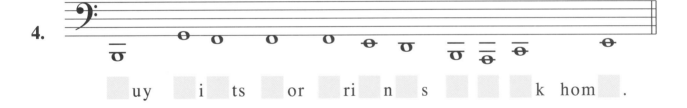

☐ uy ☐ i ☐ ts ☐ or ☐ ri ☐ n ☐ s ☐ ☐ k hom ☐ .

Use with Lesson Book 4, pg. 37

Farewell

As their visit ends, Spike and Party Cat board the plane bound for home. It has been a great trip, and they have many memories to share with friends back home.

Name the notes below to recall some of the places they visited in *Music City*.

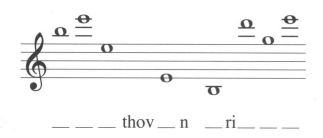

Gr__n__ St_____ St____ium

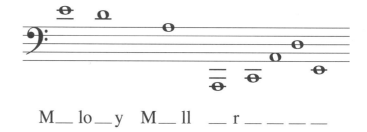

M__lo__y M__ll __r_____

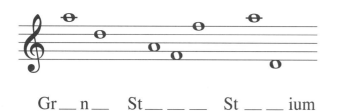

_____ thov__n __ri_____

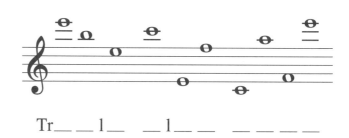

Tr____l__ __l____ _____

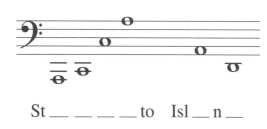

St_____ to Isl__n__

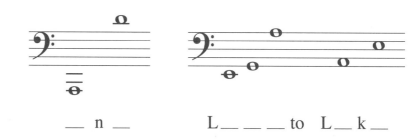

__n__   L_____ to L__k__